D1077829

44139000238430

Dedication – For Faye Pirotta
For John Hodgson, with love – S.A.

Text copyright © 2001 Sam Godwin
Illustrations copyright © 2001 Simone Abel
Volume copyright © 2001 Hodder Wayland

Series concept and design: Liz Black
Book design: Jane Hawkins
Commissioning Editor: Lisa Edwards
Editor: Katie Orchard
Science Consultant: Dr Carol Ballard

Published in Great Britain in 2001 as Rise and Shine by Hodder Wayland,
an imprint of Hodder Children's Books

This paperback edition published in 2009 by Wayland,
an imprint of Hachette Children's Books,
338 Euston Road, London NW1 3BH
www.hachettelivre.co.uk

The right of Sam Godwin to be identified as the author
and the right of Simone Abel to be identified as the
illustrator of this Work has been asserted by them in
accordance with the Copyright, Designs and Patents Act 1988.

All rights reserved. No part of this publication may be reproduced,
stored in a retrieval system, or transmitted, in any form or by any
means without the prior written permission of the publisher, nor
be otherwise circulated in any form of binding or cover other
than that in which it is published and without a similar condition
being imposed on the subsequent purchaser.

Cataloguing in publication data
Sam Godwin
From Sunrise to Sunset: a first look at light. – (Little Bees)
1. Light
I. Title
535

ISBN 978 07502 5881 4

Printed and bound in China

From Sunrise to Sunset

A first look at light

From Sunrise to Sunset

A first look at light

Sam Godwin

WAYLAND

It is very early in the morning.

Up with the larks, dear.

Soon the sun rises. Some animals wake up.

Flowers start to open.

In the sunlight everything looks

Wow! It's so bright, Mummy.

10

bright and colourful.

Don't look straight at the sun, dear. It will hurt your eyes.

Where did that worm go?

11

A big cloud floats across the sky.

It hides the sun.

The sun shines brightly again.

That's not a light, dear. It's the sun's reflection.

Who's that handsome frog in there?

15

The sun shines behind a tree. It makes a big shadow.

16

It's the end of the day.

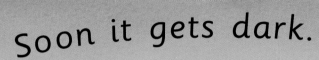

Soon it gets dark.

People can't see as well as cats in the dark.

People turn on the lights...

So that's why they need to have the lights on!

When it's dark, people can also use

At night, the moon shines in the sky.

I can see lots of different lights from here.

Some are near and some are far away.

Soon the sun will rise again.

It will be another day.

Oh, no!
Not again!

Useful Words

Moon

The moon travels around the Earth. It has no light of its own. It reflects some of the light from the sun.

Reflection

An image that can be seen in a shiny surface, such as a mirror or still water in a pool.

Shadow

When light shines behind an object, it makes a shadow – a dark shape.

Sun

The sun is a star around which the Earth travels.It gives us light and warmth.

Important

The sun's rays are very strong, so:

• Always wear sun cream when you are out in the sun.

• Never look straight at the sun. It will hurt your eyes.

All about light

If something covers the sun, we can't see it any more. But it's still there.

Light from the sun makes things look bright and colourful.

We can't see the sun at night.

There are lots of different sources of light.

Shiny surfaces reflect light.